Queen Elizabeth II

A Little Golden Book® Biography

W0114180

By Jen Arena
Illustrated by Monique Dong

 A GOLDEN BOOK • NEW YORK

Text copyright © 2022 by Jen Arena
Cover art and interior illustrations copyright © 2022 by Monique Dong
All rights reserved. Published in the United States by Golden Books, an imprint of Random
House Children's Books, a division of Penguin Random House LLC, 1745 Broadway, New
York, NY 10019. Golden Books, A Golden Book, A Little Golden Book, the G colophon, and
the distinctive gold spine are registered trademarks of Penguin Random House LLC.
rhcbooks.com
Educators and librarians, for a variety of teaching tools, visit us at RHTeachersLibrarians.com
Library of Congress Control Number: 2021941340
ISBN 978-0-593-48012-0 (trade) — ISBN 978-0-593-48013-7 (ebook)
Printed in the United States of America
10 9 8 7 6

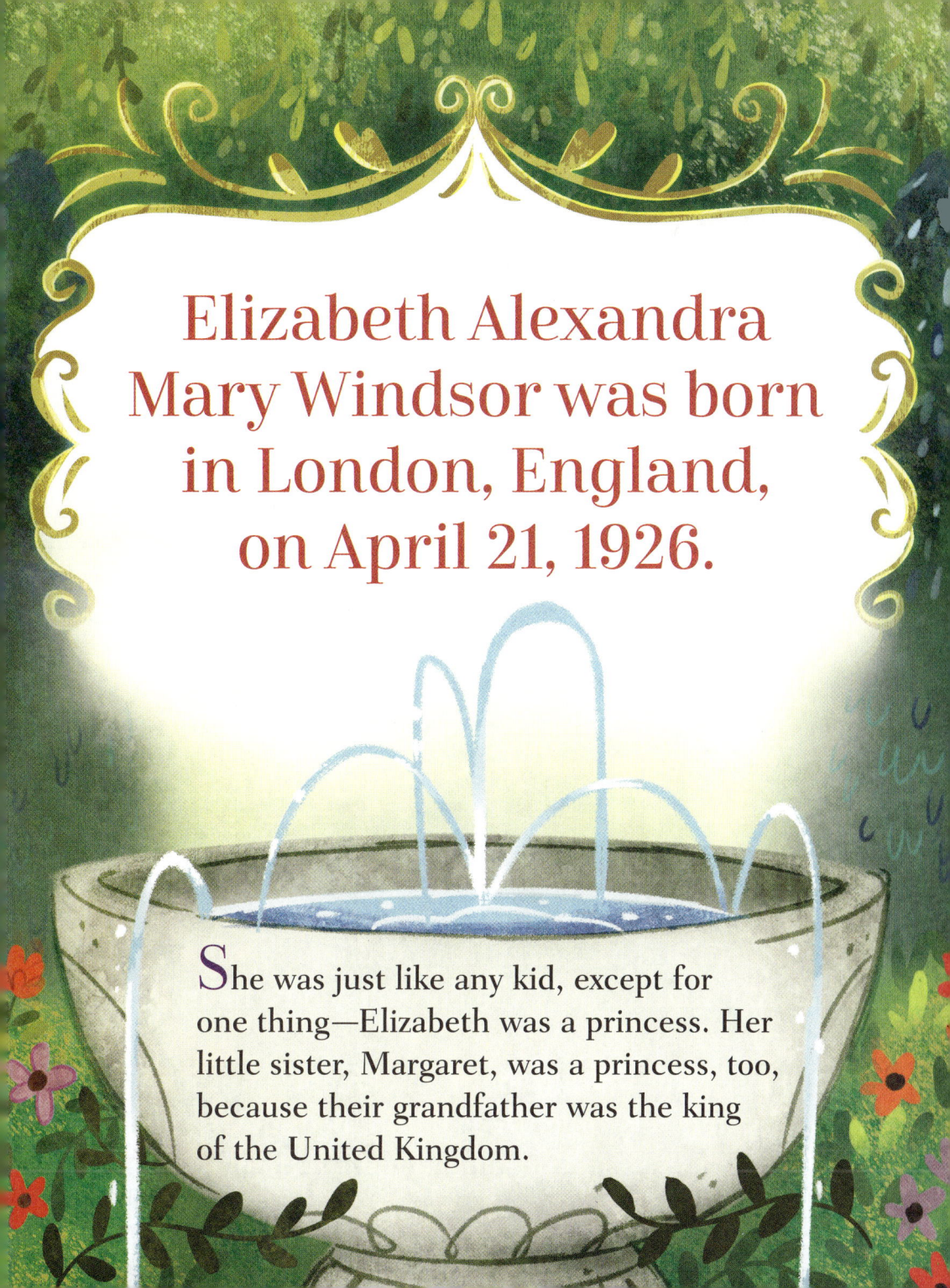

Elizabeth Alexandra Mary Windsor was born in London, England, on April 21, 1926.

She was just like any kid, except for one thing—Elizabeth was a princess. Her little sister, Margaret, was a princess, too, because their grandfather was the king of the United Kingdom.

Elizabeth and Margaret first lived in a town house in London. It had twenty-five bedrooms and a ballroom, but it wasn't a palace.

Lilibet—that was Elizabeth's nickname—was smart, a little shy, and very organized! Before bedtime, she lined up her toy horses and pretended to feed them.

The girls didn't go to school. They had lessons at home.

Their family was close and happy. No one thought Elizabeth and Margaret's father would ever be king. Their uncle, his brother, was next in line to the throne.

When Elizabeth was ten years old, everything changed. Her grandfather passed away and her uncle became king . . . but only for a short time. Now suddenly, Elizabeth's father had to be king. Since he didn't have a son, his oldest child, Elizabeth, was his heir to the throne. One day she would be the queen!

The family moved into Buckingham Palace. The king didn't make the laws of the land—that power belonged to Parliament. Still, Britain's ruler had an important role, and Elizabeth's father wanted her to be prepared. He taught her to feel a sense of duty. Elizabeth grew up believing that she served the people, not that the people served her.

In 1939, Hitler's army invaded Poland, which started World War II. The king and queen stayed in Buckingham Palace even as it was bombed. For safety, the two princesses lived at Windsor Castle in the countryside. The crown jewels were hidden there, too, sixty feet under the castle—in a biscuit tin!

"And when **peace** comes, remember it will be for us, the children of today,

During the war, Princess Elizabeth wanted to help. She raised money for the troops. She gave a radio speech to cheer up children like her, who were away from home because of the war.

to make the **World** of tomorrow a better and happier place."

In 1945, when she was eighteen, Elizabeth signed up for the women's branch of the British Army. She learned to change tires, strip an engine, and drive large trucks.

On the day the war ended, crowds of people cheered and danced in the streets outside Buckingham Palace. Princess Elizabeth and Princess Margaret happily joined them!

After the war, things didn't get better right away. London had been bombed and would need to be rebuilt.

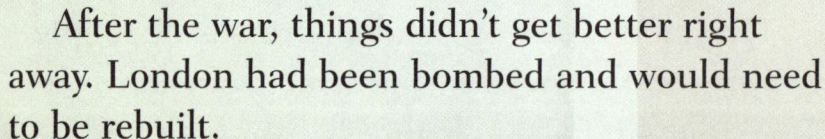

But soon came some happy news—a royal wedding! Elizabeth was in love. She had met charming, handsome Philip when she was just eight years old.

They'd met again when she was thirteen, and for years, they had written letters back and forth. On November 20, 1947, they got married.

Sadly, Elizabeth's father passed away a few years later. Elizabeth, her family, and the country mourned the king.

When she was just twenty-five years old, Elizabeth rode to Westminster Abbey in a fancy gold coach pulled by eight horses. Wearing a white satin dress and a plush purple robe, she swore to govern with justice and mercy. A heavy crown was placed on her head.

England had a new queen, Elizabeth II!

Queen Elizabeth didn't wear a robe and a crown every day. She mostly wore colorful suits and hats. But every day, she served the people and her country.

She raised a family, too. Elizabeth and Philip had four children—three boys and one girl.

Years passed, and then decades. Calm, steady Queen Elizabeth kept watch over her country.

By tradition, the queen stayed out of politics. She didn't even vote! But that didn't mean she didn't make changes.

She became friends with Nelson Mandela and supported his work against racism in South Africa.

She visited Ireland, despite its troubled history with Britain. She was the first British ruler to go there in one hundred years.

She backed a new British law allowing a ruler's oldest child—a son or a daughter—to be heir to the throne.

Being queen wasn't always easy. Queen Elizabeth once famously said that 1992 was a horrible year. Her children, now grown, were unhappy. Her heir, Prince Charles, separated from his wife, Princess Diana. Then Windsor Castle caught fire!

Slowly, things settled down. Her grandchildren got married and had children of their own.

In 2012, Britain celebrated something very special—a Diamond Jubilee. Elizabeth had been queen for sixty years! There were concerts, fireworks, and picnics. People lined the streets to cheer. With her family around her, Queen Elizabeth watched and waved . . . and smiled.

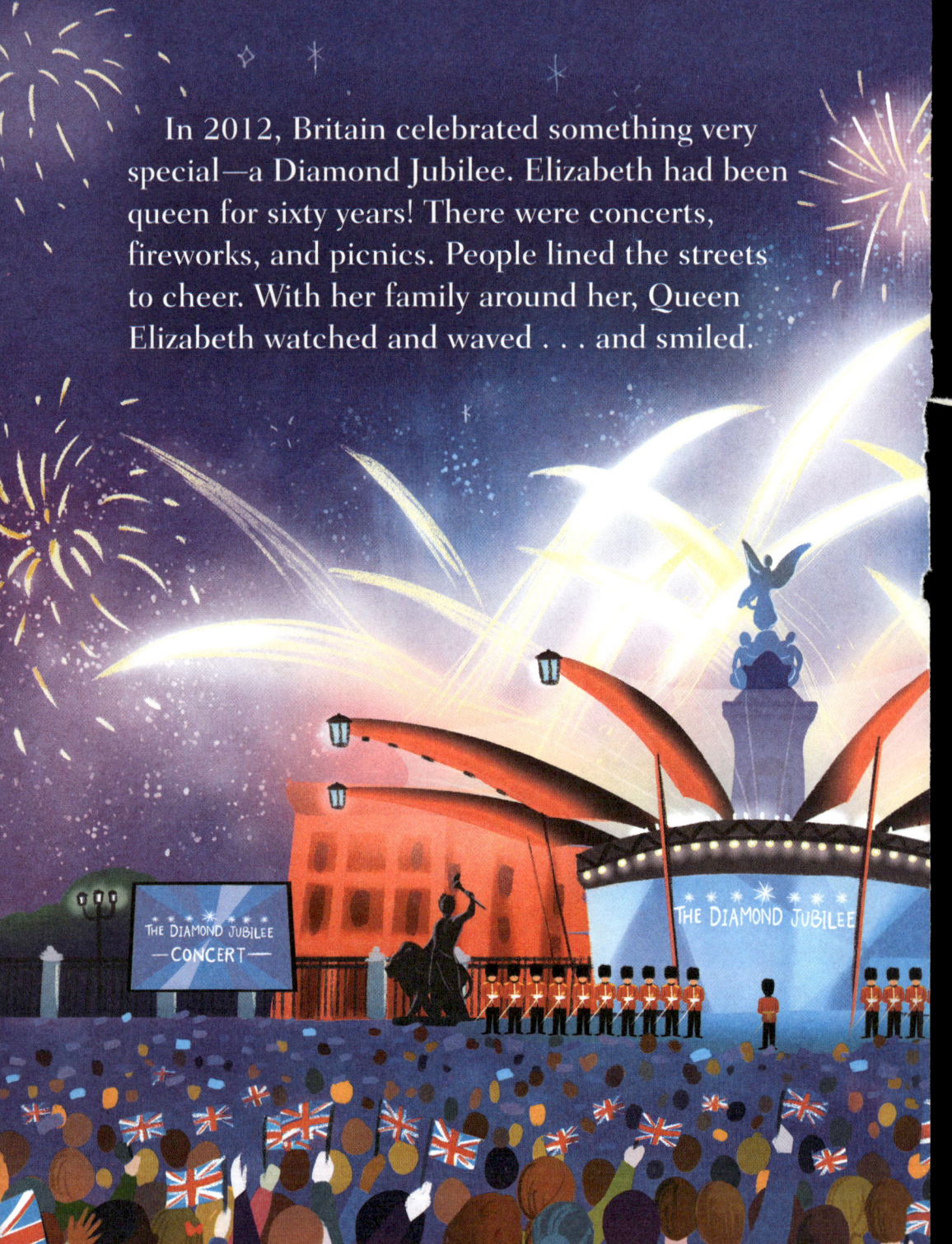

A few years later, on September 9, 2015, Queen Elizabeth II became Britain's longest-ruling monarch, overtaking her great-great-grandmother Queen Victoria's record. And in 2022, Elizabeth marked seventy years on the throne. To honor her, Britain threw its first Platinum Jubilee!

That same year, the Queen died on September 8, and her long reign ended. She was ninety-six years old.

THE DIAMOND JUBILEE —CONCERT—

In war and in peace, in good times and bad, Queen Elizabeth carried on. Fate had made her a queen. And by working hard, she won the people's respect. She always put the crown and the country above everything.

And the country's crown had no brighter jewel.